Undogumented

My Year as a Foster Dog Mom

A Memoir

Anita Corsi

For my family, my friends, and all dog lovers

ISBN: 978-1-7778008-0-2

Edited and Formatted by Self-Publishing Services LLC.

SELF-PUBLISHING SERVICES LLC
HELPING YOU WITH ALL YOUR PUBLISHING NEEDS

www.SelfPublishingServices.com

Table of Contents

Prologue

I have always felt passionate about animal rescue—specifically dog rescue. Never have I really acted on that passion until now. I mean, when I was a child, I used to try to save worms from getting crushed by vehicle tires when it rained and they were all out on the pavement. I think I was really just trying to find a way to pass the time while my dad, who was a teacher, made me stand out on bus duty with him each morning before school.

Dogs (and many other animals) are helpless and quick to trust, which is why we need to do our part in protecting them. I truly believe we were given authority over this planet so that we could live in harmony with all of creation by nourishing it and being nourished by it.

It wasn't until my dad told me about three years ago that we would start fostering dogs that I realized people can actually do that. He had a connection with someone in a local animal rescue organization and had initially wanted to do it for my two-year-old niece, who was the first grandchild in the family and adored dogs. My dad was allergic to animal hair, so we could only accept hypoallergenic breeds. It was a unique experience and we fostered only two dogs, but they were easygoing and happy-go-lucky.

I quickly learned the concept of fostering. It's the process of ensuring the animals' physical, emotional, and mental baggage is treated before they are sent to a forever home. It is also the process where you discover which characteristics of a forever home are best-suited for the dogs and their growth. Even though we're not keeping the dogs, we get to play a part in the restorative process, which is really special. It's so fulfilling to know you've provided a nurturing and stable environment and now they get to go off to the perfect home—

to someone who will love them and provide what's best for them for the long term. There is so much meaning in this closure. It's about giving the animals a chance to be at peace in a comfortable environment and preparing them for a permanent home with minimal anxiety. Maybe you could say it's like raising your kids and then watching them go off to live a better life. It just makes you happy to see them go live their best life. And you just want to make the decision that's best for the dog. My mindset all along has been to take a dog in, love it and help it, send it to a better place, and repeat. And that's what helps me do what I do.

The thing with any dog—I guess I should say most dogs—is that they're not hard to please. They just need a home and someone who will take care of and love them, just like humans do. Knowing that brings peace to the process of letting go, especially when you've met the new parents and experienced how much joy and love radiates from them when they're in the dog's presence.

When I moved out, I could finally have all the dogs I wanted, whether they shed or not. But then I realized I couldn't afford them and remembered that fostering a dog is just like having a free one, with all expenses paid, except it is just temporary. So I contacted the organization, had a couple interviews, and I was good to go. Little did I know this journey would be a lot more than just having a free dog and the happy-go-lucky lifestyle I had anticipated.

Chapter One: Roo

You know that thing you had as a kid that you believed you could never live without? Your blankie, stuffed animal, or whatever gave you the most comfort? Well, that was my miniature poodle, Taffy, for 14 years of my life. I was made fun of in elementary school for loving her so much. I literally wrote her name (surrounded by hearts) on every single book I owned. We always said we would spread her ashes at the local beach. Fast-forward to three years after her death: We still haven't had the strength to touch them. I remember walking at the beach shortly after she passed and walking past a woman carrying a small dog that looked like a miniature poodle. I asked if I could pet her dog and as soon as I approached her, I started bawling my eyes out. She was understanding, and I'm sorry to have put someone in that position, but sometimes you just need to allow yourself to feel your emotions.

Fortunately, my first foster dog was a big version of Taffy. Same soft touch, same chocolate nose, same smell. It was so comforting to get to feel her and kiss her again in a different form. Except this dog was a wreck. She was said to have been verbally abused, but it was obvious she had had it much worse. Roo was dropped off at our house on April 12, 2019. She was so frightened by everything. When she first entered our house, she dropped down in our hallway and did not move for hours. I was too nervous to approach her for the first day because of how afraid she was, and I wasn't sure if she would attack me out of defense.

Her name was Hadley, but we called her Roo. The organization was unsure of her breed, but she must have been a goldendoodle or something similar. She was two years old and terrified of people she didn't know. At first, I didn't know what to call her because I assumed that her next owner would change her name anyway, so I resorted to saying, "Come here, dog." I felt like Sandra Bullock's character from *Bird Box,* who called the children in her care "Girl" and "Boy."

To the left is my Taffy girl. Roo is on the right.

At the beginning it seems like fun and games to have a free dog with no commitment, but Roo taught us that it's much more than that. Dogs are vulnerable creatures and some, like Roo, experience an abuse of the power they so freely give us. Even though some may be physically stronger than we are, they submit to us and let us have dominion over them—the most humbling characteristic of a dog. It was not about fun and games when Roo came into our lives. It was about giving this creature with such a mysterious past a chance to trust us and a chance to live up to her true potential.

She slowly became comfortable as we talked to her and approached her gently over the next few days. The most difficult challenge was walking her down my street. Every little noise, movement, and person in the distance spiked her anxiety and she would try to take off. It was as if every sound triggered a PTSD flashback and she interpreted the noises of vehicles and people as personal attacks. She was strong, and it was impossible to get her comfortable enough to go to the bathroom. I became so fed up with having my arms pulled out of their sockets that I tried wrapping her leash around my waist.

When that didn't work, I tried a harness, which usually does work. However, it didn't with Roo, so I used a halti, a type of harness that goes around a dog's muzzle. That worked terrifically. She got free once when I tried the harness and she ran quickly down my road. I was terrified that I would lose her. Nothing mattered but getting her back. I dropped her leash and everything in my hands and booked it. Some people came out of their houses to help me chase her. She was so fast that I didn't see where she ended up, so I started racing back home with my heart pounding out of my chest. There she was at the door. She knew where her only solace was, and that made me feel relief and satisfaction. I knew then that we finally belonged to each other.

The more time you invest in caring for something, the more valuable it becomes to you.

Some people think dogs need to be disciplined for every little transgression, but I think we need to let them just be dogs. Like people, they can't read our minds and they will never be perfect. But if we allow them to be themselves, prioritize their needs, discipline them when they do something bad, but reward them even more when they do something right, then we will finally deserve and experience them at their best. When one has freedom, one has the opportunity to flourish and reach full potential. When freedom is taken away, that life inside goes dormant.

It took a while for Roo to trust us. She never even barked or made one sound. When we invited company in, she would hide behind the couch or under the bed and tremble. We had to slowly accustom her to their presence before she grew excited to see familiar faces. My partner, Jacob, came into the house once with a hood on; as he approached her, she cowered as if she expected to be struck. It wasn't until he started talking that she recognized him and immediately perked up and wagged her tail. My heart sank deep, and I felt so sad thinking about the life she had once had—a life I will never be told about. It's a shame dogs can't speak of their pasts. They just reveal it through tiny subtleties in their behaviour.

We had to be patient, but once she developed the self-esteem to reveal her true personality, it was all worth it. Dogs are like humans in that their potential will flourish only if they have self-esteem. And it's up to their owner to allow them to develop their self-esteem. Here are some of the adorable positions we would often find her in.

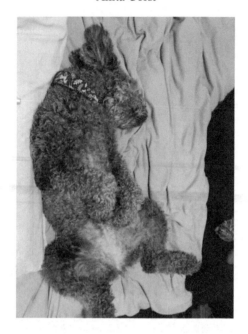

Roo loved carrots. She devoured them. After her, I couldn't get another dog to eat a carrot ever again. She wasn't really into toys, but she did love to wrestle in bed. She quickly grew curious about us and became a great family dog when we all got together. She was the perfect jogging companion for my sister, and my dad used to bounce her in his arms while music was playing. Everyone loved her, and she was great with my niece. She came home after being groomed one day and was a completely different dog. It was scary but hilarious. She went from a giant plush teddy bear to a giant naked mole rat.

Jacob would not allow her to sleep in bed with us, and Roo knew very well that she would get pushed off. She would wait until he left for work every morning and jump up and sleep beside me until I woke up. She also had a habit of licking where he slept and creating a huge patch of soaked sheets. I just stopped caring and let it air-dry without really telling Jacob...oops. Maybe that's why he was developing skin rashes. Hmm.

I mentioned that I never heard her bark or make a sound. I have also never seen a dog run as fast as she could. I took her to the local dog park regularly. As soon as I let her off leash, she would take off, running and spinning in large circles, taking full advantage of the freedom provided to her by the large stretch of grass. It filled me with joy to see the happiness radiating from her as she gallivanted and pounced around. Then we'd come home and she'd spend hours lying on the shower floor. I assume she enjoyed how cool it felt. It made it difficult to take a shower when there was a dog sprawled out, living her best life with no desire to compromise it anytime soon.

We used to take her to Jacob's dad's house in the country and play hide-and-seek in the tall grass. When she was far enough away from us, we would hide and watch her return, sniff around, and zoom through the grass to find us. It was a challenge she enjoyed, and she would embrace us victoriously when she finally ran into us.

Roo was the dog we had for the longest time. She left us on September 10, after five months. A few days before that, we had a meet-and-greet with a couple who wanted her. She had received a handful of applications, but the organization was very picky as to who would be a perfect match. The couple was in love with Roo and wanted her immediately. Before we met up a few days later, I let her lick some of my homemade tomato sauce off a plate. It was her well-earned treat and last little spoiling that I could get in before she left me forever.

We all felt good about the decision. The couple drove off with Roo, and I remember thinking that it was probably much easier for a dog to be picked up by their new owners than to be dropped off and left at a stranger's house. The new parents have been amazing and still send me updates a year later. It makes me so proud to see how happy she is in her forever home.

She has become a sassy little drama queen, but she is happy. No more holding back and no more hiding in distress. She is still wary of new people, which may never go away. She was prepared to trust her new parents quickly because she had come a long way with us—five months of learning to trust people again. It was extremely rewarding and a difficult couple weeks for us in our empty house afterward.

Roo is living proof that if we treat dogs right, we will reap the benefits of a companionship like no other. We can show humanity by taking care of the things we were blessed with in this life. Nothing we have is truly ours; we are just borrowing it while we're here. We aren't entitled to anything so it's important to be grateful for the things given into our care. And I know she is being adored by her new amazing parents.

To this day, my dad still talks about how he wishes he had kept Roo. Anytime we mention dogs, he says, "Roo would have been great for that." Okay, well, Roo was so last year. Get over it already.

Photo by Jacob Ellison. 2019.

Fun Fact: According to Sheila McClear, author of the article, "Those Cute Labradoodles Mask a Dark, Disturbing Truth," in the *New York Post*, poodle mixes shed minimally if at all, so they are great companions for those who are typically allergic to dogs and cats.

Not-so-fun Fact: McClear also shares that high demand for this breed has driven success for puppy mills with corrupt practices. It is best to adopt any breed from a shelter or a reputable breeder.

Chapter Two: Paco

I had learned from Roo that, going forward, I would have to be patient. Instead of getting discouraged right away if things are not going smoothly, I must give the dog time to trust me. It doesn't require much from me—

just that I am consistent with the dog and accommodating. All dogs really need is a loving home with someone who provides them food, water, attention, and exercise. It can be simple or complex, depending on the dog's specific needs and personality, but it should be consistent. Consistency and stability breed trust.

I was notified about Paco a month after Roo left. As much as we missed Roo, it was nice having a little break and I knew she was living her best life. Paco was a five-year-old, white husky mix who shed a LOT. He did have the most handsome face, my gosh. His face resembled a pit bull/husky mix—pure white with deep black eyes and light brown freckles on his ears and nose. I picked him up on October 1.

I had heard something from the organization about how dogs had to be restrained while being transported in a car but I thought, "Nah it's okay. How would I even do that?" Then I quickly regretted not investigating that responsibility further. I put him in the front seat and started driving home. He was extremely happy-go-lucky, but it wasn't just his tail going crazy. He was standing up, moving around, leaning and sliding his front legs across the dashboard. My car and I were covered in white hairs. The part that gave me a heart attack was when I turned into my driveway and almost hit my neighbor's parked truck because Paco decided to take over the steering wheel and sit on my lap. I couldn't help but laugh loudly at how ridiculously things had escalated, and I made a major mental note never to let him ride shotgun again.

Paco always waltzed right in the house with the same giddiness as he left it. He was very well-behaved. He was rescued from a high-kill pound in Quebec. It is so sad to think that such an energetic dog with such a big personality was among many others who were all going to have their lives extinguished. And it's even more devastating to think about all the ones that actually don't get rescued in time.

I would compare Paco to Roo, and I was a little bitter toward him for the first couple days because of the things he didn't do that Roo would do—like running at the dog park. He didn't seem to have much interest in running. He did like to explore though. Funny how it started this way but ended with him being my favourite of all the dogs I had fostered. Well, at least until the fifth dog came along, but we will get to that later.

Paco was the first dog I created a promotional video for. One of my favourite hobbies is to create homemade videos, so I created a short music video of clips of him so that potential adopters could get a sense of his personality. He was incredibly sweet, always smiling; he always attacked me in the morning with his joyful greetings. He loved to cuddle, and he loved trying to eat flies. He would jump up and contort his body so he could snatch them up with his mouth. It was very entertaining.

We took him to an adoption event at a local pet store. He was restless, so we bought him a brand-new white sheep toy. Within fifteen minutes, the squeaker was out, the sheep was mutilated, its white fur was brown, and strings were dangling from the ripped sides. You'd think we had had this toy passed around from dog to dog for years. Unlike Roo, Paco absolutely adored toys.

Car rides consisted of him sitting in the back seat, tied up. He would still manage to get his head up close to mine by squeezing it between the passenger seat and the door when I wasn't driving. One time, he managed to squeeze his two front legs through that crack just to be close to me. He looked so silly, but it made me love him more. He had this screeching cry that he would let out until I started petting him and holding his head close to mine.

Paco was so demanding and had so much energy that we tried not to let him have any rest all day so he'd sleep through the night. One day, we kept him alert at all times and would not allow him to lie down or rest. Then we had a movie night and he sat there throughout the movie, bobbing his head and leaning over because he couldn't stay awake. It was funny to witness and a nice accomplishment to finally have him tired out for the night. Another way to drain his energy was by using a laser light. It turns out it's not only cats that are crazy about that light. He would chase it all over the house for as long as we allowed him to.

I can't imagine the everyday mundanity of life without the sweet presence of a dog. There's a major difference between waking up to make myself a tea, sitting down at the laptop with my mind wandering, thinking about my objectives or obligations and waking up to a little (or big) creature that eagerly greets me, takes me for a refreshing walk, then lounges around with me and gives me cuddles in between my work. This has a relaxing, destressing, and rejuvenating effect. I know it sounds personal, but I think many dog owners understand this difference. In my experience, dogs help prevent me from feeling depressed or having a wandering mind. Dogs help take your mind off of yourself and notice what's right in front of you, to nurture it and be nurtured by it. It can be good to have a wandering, reflective mind but it is important to snap out of it every now and then and be present where you are, taking in the temporary moments. We have been offered a creature of another species that is connecting with us in real time, and that is amazing.

Photo by Jacob Ellison. 2019.

It's the small things that impact us the most. The memories and the feelings are the things that count.

I was so excited to be on my second foster dog; I felt like I could label myself a real foster dog mom. I wanted to take it up a notch and try having more than one dog at a time—ideally two or three, so I talked to the organization about it. I wanted that full family feeling. That's when I got the next two. Paco was great with them. He would even slow down to their pace when we were all on a walk together. He was only there for the first week after we got them and then he was sent to his forever home. I had taken him to an event at a farm where I met the couple who fell in love with him. They had big dreams for him. When I took him over for a home visit, he was completely distracted by their two big cats, making it his life's mission to follow them all around the house. I knew he would never be bored there.

This was the first time I drove the dog right to the new parents' home, although I did learn afterward that it's not ideal. I actually cried when I was driving him over to their house for good. Coincidentally, *Big Girls Don't Cry* by Fergie was playing on the car radio and made me feel even more emotional. I hadn't cried for Roo, and I figured it would be easier since I had gotten past the first dog. But no. It may get easier to let other people take them, but missing them does not get easier.

When we ran into Paco months later, he was so healthy-looking and happy. They had a big yard for him to enjoy. He left us after one month exactly, on November 1. I had already started my next adventure.

Photo by Jacob Ellison. 2019.

Fun Fact: In the article, "10 Warm Facts About Huskies" by Rebecca O'Connell from the *Mental Floss* magazine, we learn that huskies were once used in armies as search and rescue dogs, and for transportation, freighting, and communication. They also share DNA with the grey wolf.

Not-so-fun Fact: An article from the *Burgess Pet Care* website reveals that many huskies are abandoned after people realize they are a lot to handle. They are most suitable to people who can devote the time and energy these dogs need and give them lots of exercise and attention, as they are working dogs.

Chapter Three: Coco and Chanel

These. Girls. Were. Psycho. So incredibly cute and sweet. But psycho. I adored them for it. On October 26, I picked them up at the local truck stop where I had picked up Paco, each in her own crate. They had flown in that morning from Mexico. I will emphasize that I did not assign them their names, but as I came to know them, I figured they really did suit their names. They were such dolls.

I believe Coco and Chanel were two tiny terrier mixes. They resembled giant hamsters, so we called them little rat dogs. Coco was black and Chanel was blonde, and they were sisters. Coco was the mature one and the leader. Chanel was the devious, adorable one with eyes bulging out of her head. During a bath, those eyes got even bulgier.

I picked them up around midnight. They were found abandoned on the rooftop of an apartment building in Mexico. The poor babies! When we got home, I just put them right in the living room and went to bed. I kid you not: The entire night, it sounded like the footsteps of a hundred hamsters wrestling and jumping all over the house. When I woke up, I was scared to see what the living room looked like. And sure enough, shoes had been tampered with, towels and toys were thrown around, their dog beds were flipped inside out, and little pee puddles and poop piles were scattered about. The girls were also able to climb on the furniture like cats! I caught Chanel with her back feet on the couch, reaching up onto the filing cabinet to get some water from the plant watering can. I couldn't be mad at her as her survival skills were quite impressive. Plus, I guess I should have given them water throughout the night...

Another time I caught her when her water bowl had been picked up.

We crated them at night after that. They entertained each other constantly, so it was very easy maintenance. Chanel was my favourite because her eyes had so much character. I really wanted to give them a bath the second day I had them because they had flown overseas and had been everywhere. I didn't have a bathtub, and I decided they were tiny enough to come in the shower with me. The poor little angels. I felt so bad. I locked them in the bathroom with me, washed one at a time, then washed myself. When I opened the curtain to come out, they were just sitting still on the floor staring at me, traumatized, as if I had just violated them. I do admit I could have waited another week until they trusted me a little bit before drenching and handling them.

It didn't take long for them to adjust—to start coming outside with me, acknowledging me with their noses and then giddily moseying around the yard with their tails straight up like they happily owned the turf.

It's always emotional when I meet a dog for the first time, knowing I'm taking them home. It's like seeing a newborn baby observe a new world for the first time. Some have been through more adverse experiences than I have in their short lives. Now they have been given a second chance at life. Some bear their traumatic experiences with bitterness and pain just like some people do. But one thing I learned from all of them is that they don't always live in the anxiety that comes with uncertainty. They live with gratitude, no matter how many places they've been shoved around and no matter what they have been given or what has been withheld from them. They overcome their misery with their enthusiasm and appreciation of the simple, good things in the present moment. Coco and Chanel were resilient. They went with the flow of change and tolerated their circumstances.

Chanel to the left and Coco to the right

My heart sinks when I think that they could have starved on that rooftop. They were so vulnerable. At my house, their tails wagged nonstop. They had the cutest little wrestling matches with each other and did these crazy little happy dances where they would slither around like giant, vigorous worms.

One day, I was having a bath alone at my parents' house, and I brought them and locked them in the bathroom with me.

I was sick and feeling weak. They were so well-behaved and quiet the whole time. When I got up and showered and drained the water, my vision blurred and I felt dizzy, so I just lay back down in the tub for a couple minutes and closed my eyes. Coco seemed to sense that something was wrong, so she moved the curtain with her nose and started whimpering while trying to assess me. It was so sweet. I told her I was okay and got up slowly. I was surprised at how intuitive she was, given that she was always focused on harassing her sister.

Coco was more reserved and didn't need much attention, although she made it clear that she liked it. She more loved tormenting her sister and portraying her dominance over her while Chanel apathetically gave in. Chanel's eyes were always on me though. She always wanted some reaction from me; she wanted me to acknowledge her. She was so intentional with those soulful eyes that I always gave in to her. She got her fair share of kisses from me on that tiny little face.

I made a promotional video for the sisters, who were to be adopted out together. Their song was *It Takes Two*, by Marvin Gaye and Kim Weston, revealing their cuddliest and most playful moments. They also seemed to love the snow, which I found interesting, considering that they probably had never seen it before. They used to sleep in their crate in the bedroom. Every morning when I shuffled in bed, I could hear their tails wagging briskly in excitement. One of the most depressing parts of giving up a dog is to lose those greetings in the morning and when you return home. Those greetings that make you feel like your existence is essential to someone. That you matter. These moments are so important in any relationship.

My supervisor at work once gave me these cheddar treats that her two dogs adored. Every time I pulled the bag out, the girls would jump up and down repetitively on their two back feet. If your treat selection can turn your dogs into little kangaroos, I think those treats are a keeper.

I heard about Coco and Chanel's future parents through the organization and went right to their house with the girls for a home visit. They were so kind and fun and had a big, fenced-in yard for the girls to frolic in. I advised the organization that they shouldn't go to a home with kids, as Chanel had a habit of barking helplessly when left alone in a room with my niece. It was sad and made me wonder what kind of troublesome experiences she had had with kids back home.

They peed a lot. On everything. I felt horrible bringing my dogs in, letting them pee and poop on a stranger's carpet, then leaving them to deal with it. But their new parents did not seem to mind. I knew they were good for the girls because that didn't seem to be a deal breaker! They understood that Coco and Chanel were house-trained; they just soil when they're in a new environment. I brought the girls for a couple more home visits where I let them spend half the day alone with the couple.

I knew one day I wouldn't have them anymore, so I needed to enjoy them while I did. Take in their smell, hold them close to me, kiss them. Fostering has really helped me realize that every moment is temporary, so we have to make the most of them. There will be a day when I will never hug them again. There will be a day when we will never hug a loved one again, which is why gratitude is so vital. We must take in every single instant fully and embrace it wholeheartedly.

When I drove them over for the last time on December 14, I was extremely emotional. I tried not to cry in front of the couple, but they could already sense my sorrow. The lady hugged me and kissed me on the cheek, which I thought was really sweet. It's a beautiful relationship to have because we both share the experience of having been mothers to the same two babies. I drove right to Walmart afterward to do some errands and bawled the entire way, reliving the moment when Chanel looked at me with those needy, betrayed, helpless eyes as I left her there. I walked into Walmart rocking my puffy, red eyes, and I just couldn't care less because I felt emotionally drained. I'm so blessed the owners kept in touch. You live with someone, take care of them, come to truly know and tolerate each other, then you let them go forever. It doesn't matter how many times you do it. It's loss. And it's bittersweet. It's mournful but in a beautiful way.

I keep reminding myself that it's okay to miss her, but when I do, to send her love and light every time I think about her, then drop it. Just like that message from *Eat, Pray, Love*. One thing you learn is that time does heal the pain that loss brings. Each time I bring a dog to its new home I remember that and think about how in a couple weeks, everything will be good and back to normal for both of us. It's the adjustment period that we often struggle with.

I arranged to meet up with the girls about a month later, and they didn't seem to remember me. We were in a public place, so their minds were pretty distracted, but Chanel had zero interest in me as I sat down, petted her, and talked to her. She only had eyes for her new mommy. I was a little heartbroken and remember going home and saying that she was just a stupid rat. It did make it much easier to let her go, knowing she didn't think she needed me anymore. But of course, she felt that way because she had amazing parents, and that's the point. That's what she deserved.

We get to experience the complete essence of joy when we have a companion to share it with.

Fun Fact: I Googled Coco Chanel and discovered from Laurel Pinson's article on *StyleCaster* that she was a businesswoman and French fashion designer who contributed to the evolution of fashion trends after World War I, bringing freedom to people to dress how they wanted. She is also known for her empowering and beautiful quotes.

Coco and Chanel were independent and upbeat, and they challenged norms. I am glad they had those names.

Not-so-fun Fact: An article from *The Yucatan Times* shares that, in 2018, it was determined that 70% of Mexico's dogs lived on the street, either disregarded by their owners or born as strays. Mexico has the largest number of street dogs in Latin America.

Chapter Four: Nacho

The fifth foster dog. The favourite. When I first saw pictures of him, I thought he was really unattractive, and zombie-like with his one brown eye and the other bright blue from a visual impairment that resembled a cataract. He was four years old and was said to have lived on the streets of Mexico his whole life, finding his own food, and never getting any help. Then he was rescued on a stormy night while standing still in the middle of vehicle flow. The lady who picked him up said he had dreadlocks that covered his eyes and face, and beneath them, he was a skeleton.

I picked him up in Oshawa the day after I said bye to Coco and Chanel. I drove him home while playing classical music and talking so he would get to know my voice and be relaxed. I had made this a habit with the previous dogs as well. It was as if the crate was empty. He had not made a single peep. I brought him in the house and tried to handle him very slowly as he was clearly not used to the human touch. I was worried about feeding him too much at once, so I started off with small portions throughout the day, accompanied by cooked potato slices (sometimes carrots or chicken) to help fatten him up. He devoured these tiny meals as if they were the last meal he would ever receive. Every time we put him on our laps, he stood there, stiff. When you touched him, you could feel his bones. The poor little boy had never been cuddled and innocently composed himself like a puppet, waiting to see what the humans would do to him next. He was very unsure of everything. But he was the most gentle, fragile creature.

He seemed so out of place and vulnerable— as if he had walked into a castle where all his dreams were coming true and he didn't know what to make of it. And he definitely displayed appreciation for it in the way he became obedient and affectionate over time. He got a long sleep the first night. He didn't seem to want the dog bed; a pile of sheets or a thin pillow on the floor was satisfactory for him. I filmed him every morning for a few days and there were major changes in behaviour.

The first morning, I greeted him by slowly petting him and he would not budge; he was not the least bit responsive. The second morning, he rolled onto his back when I got out of bed and let me rub his tummy while he yawned. On the third morning, he actually got up and shook himself and came to me, wagging his tail, and jumped up to put his paws on my leg. He had been so weak on the first day, but it was evident that each day he was gaining a little more energy. He had become sweet and snuggly by the third day, revealing a bit more of his personality and proving that there was indeed life in that body. He confided in us fairly quickly. I believe it's because dogs always choose to see the best in us. They have faith in humans. They always carry themselves with hope.

Our wounds and scars are nothing less than beautiful accolades of perseverance.

Nacho was a very popular name among the Mexican dogs, and we were getting tired of it, so we started calling him Budgee. It just happened. Then, somehow he was getting called Mr. Bigglesworth from Austin Powers, which got shortened to Mr. B. (Dogs have this way of bringing out the silliness in you.) He was too cute for any of those names, and actually, his new owners changed his name to Buddy, which I love. I wish I had called him that from the start.

The first day he was home alone, I came home on my lunch break and was surprised to see that he had been rummaging through the recycling. Tinfoil was ripped up everywhere along with plastic bags. That was a lesson to put dirty tinfoil in the garbage (which is apparently where it belongs anyway). I realized in that moment that this had been Buddy's lifestyle back home. This was all he knew. He had to scavenge for survival. My sister also made a point that perhaps he was so quiet because he had had to avoid attention from predators on the streets. Anyway, that tinfoil was clearing his digestive system for days after, as I got to witness.

Buddy was silent and calm. Silence itself is a language. It is wonderful when two species can understand each other without speaking. It's a language that focuses on each other and on the moment. A language not consumed by thoughts of the past, or of the future, of things happening, or of responsibilities. Animals and their silence remind us to simply be.

Who would have known he would become the biggest suck-up? He put his paw up if he wanted to be petted, and I used this trick to get him to give me high fives. He was obviously very comfortable outside and such a good walker. At family get- togethers, he walked around quietly the whole time with his tail straight up, perfectly content. He finally had the comfort of a family for the first time in his life; he knew he would always get to come back to a warm home with food. He got the most worked up out of all the dogs when Jacob played with him. He would get extremely playful, zoom around in circles, and jump in weird positions. You wouldn't think a dog could contort its body in such a way. We noticed him getting to a healthy weight around three weeks in. By the time we got rid of him, he was nice and filled out.

Buddy was my favourite because in his eyes, you could see a pure, gentle soul as if he had the wisdom of an old man and a mysterious past. He looked at everyone with those tranquil eyes— eyes that are quick to trust and eyes that intentionally look into yours for a mutual connection.

Humans have many faces, but an animal's heart can be seen in their eyes.

We gave Buddy a chance to restore his youth and live the childhood he never got to have. It's like when kids have to grow up too quickly and don't get to have a childhood; he underwent a similar journey on the streets and got to be a baby again with us. He seemed to take advantage of this when he yelped bloody murder if his paw got stepped on by accident. It was a little overdramatic. My heart would jump, I would look down, and he would be relaxed, as if nothing happened. Dogs are probably the only creatures who forgive just as quickly as they get angry—a skill that even humans struggle to acquire.

I met his forever parents at a meet-and-greet event. They were so friendly and so great with him. I went for a home visit and spent two hours conversing with them in their living room. Buddy and his new father were getting along great with the toys. He didn't really seem to want to leave. I knew it was a great match, but it was also so hard to let him go. The couple made it a pleasant experience. In fact, they spoiled us with a gift card to a restaurant, along with a beautiful, sweet card including a letter thanking us for our kindness, time, and work, which was incredibly touching. They said we could visit anytime. I still see him and his new father out for lots of walks, and Buddy's tail is always perking straight up. It was rough when I dropped him off on the 25th of February, 2020. I had had him for over two months, and I felt like I was giving a big part of my heart away. I was sad about him for a long time.

It's so funny how these dogs that spent their whole life alone surviving are so snuggly. It must be a need we all share. When I think about the extensive journeys they've been on, I feel so honoured that they end up in my home. In my arms. In little Anita's home in her small town, to brighten up her small, little world.

To be blessed is to have someone in your life who is difficult to part ways with.

I looked at Buddy, into that gentle soul as he softly approached me with trust and gratitude in his eyes. So many dogs are neglected and lack the care they need—especially on the streets, like Buddy. But his spirit was not broken.

Fun Fact: According to Zoe Miller's article in *Insider,* a study conducted at Azabu University in Japan found that the love hormone, oxytocin, is produced when an owner locks eyes with their dog. Researchers analyzed oxytocin levels in people's urine after a half-hour of interaction with their dog. Cool, eh? I finally understand why Buddy has always been my favourite. He was the one dog with an eye impediment, yet his eye contact was the most meaningful. I think it was his vulnerability and his ability to trust in the midst of uncertainty—that, and he would just sit there and let me kiss his face off with all the patience in the world.

Not-so-fun Fact: In Mexico, many unwanted litters from nonspayed pets are discarded on the streets, in referring to Jessica Barrett's article on the *World Footprints* website. Fortunately, there are clinics now that perform free spay and neuter programs, making a long-term impact by helping prevent unwanted pets. They also commit to educating communities about the importance of sterilization.

Chapter Five: Bentley

I laugh when I think about how you can notice the cultural differences between dogs. I haven't had a lot of experience, but I have learned that these Mexican dogs who come from a place of suffering, loneliness, and neglect show a deep appreciation of the life we give them, whereas some Canadian dogs who have been spoiled all their lives carry a specific sass and a sense of entitlement. It's kind of funny, but Bentley was Canadian and was a tiny rodent who carried a mighty attitude.

Buddy was still in the picture when we picked up Bentley on January 21. And Bentley actually left a week before Buddy. You would think with this smaller new housemate, Buddy would take some responsibility, but he seemed to think he could follow Bentley's lead every time he peed in the house and just unlearn what we had taught him about being civilized. There was now a Mr. B and a Mini B, who was also black and four years old. We got them to play tug-of-war to keep them occupied, even though they would both just stand still and wait for the other to make a move. It made for a lot of built-up suspense with no end.

Bentley was cute, resembling Stitch from *Lilo & Stitch*, but terribly possessive. If he was sitting on my lap or touching me at all, he had this strange behaviour of growling ferociously at Jacob every time he walked by. The poor dog got a couple scoldings but never relented. His growls only got louder and fiercer. Then he would hide under the bed, and I'd be too scared to grab him because he would have me convinced that he was going to turn into a rageful lion.

He was aggressive toward me once when my niece was visiting and I reached to touch her. That behaviour was the reason he was let go by his previous owner, a lady who had a home daycare. He was extremely attached to her, but he was overprotective of the kids and would growl at her and the children's parents, so she had to give him up. She was heartbroken, of course. I knew it would be hard to find the perfect home, but he needed to be somewhere with one single lady who didn't have children in her home. This, I felt, would be the only environment where he would be truly happy.

That home was quickly found. I wasn't surprised; he had incredible charm and appeal because of his tiny, teacup figure. I must admit, I loved the excessive attention he gave me all the time. But the sooner he left my house, the better because he was not going to flourish in my home.

I met his new mommy at the same time and place I met Buddy's parents. I had taken both dogs to the event, and Bentley's new mom fell head over heels in love with him. He seemed very happy in her arms as well. She was ready to take him immediately. So, on February 22, I drove him over. Sadly, and surprisingly, he didn't want me to leave his side. He was a like a shy boy begging his mommy not to leave him in this stranger's home. I felt so bad, but I knew he would take to her quickly and become obsessed with her as he had with me.

He tried to take a poop in her house. She was sweet and didn't mind, but then he got constipated and it just wasn't going through to completion so we took him into the kitchen and took turns trying to clean him with a wet cloth. Of course, there could not have been a more terrible timing for this occurrence.

You start a new season and leave the previous one behind. You take what you learned and you do better the next time around.

People ask how we do it, foster without failing. (A foster fail is a situation where the foster parent ends up adopting the dog rather than sending him to another home.) The key is appreciating and valuing the transitional role that foster parents play. The dog that adoptive parents meet is not always the same dog that the foster parents met. The dog has undergone a transformation, whether big or small, and that's what keeps me going. It's rewarding. It's life-changing for the dogs and even for me, as each and every single one of them brings new meaning and bears profound teachings about life.

Fun Fact: If you're looking for an easy-maintenance, cuddly dog who ADORES attention, the teacup is your calling. They're like live accessories. You think an Elf on the Shelf is cute? Try a teacup poodle on your shelf.

Not-so-fun Fact: In 2018, out of all dogs in Canada's humane societies and shelters, 11% were euthanized and 47% were adopted. Fortunately, the adoption rate is continuing in an upward trend and the proportion of dogs who are euthanized is becoming much lower. This information and other interesting facts can be found in the *2018 Animal Shelter Statistics* online document.

Chapter Six: Trixie

The Mexican goddess. She was our first puppy, about six months old, and she possessed a kind of intelligence, grace, and beauty that drew lots of comments from strangers. She came in a litter from a shelter in Mexico, and her name was actually Gaga. Yes, like Lady Gaga. With her in the litter were Madonna, Beyonce, and Pink. I didn't think it could get any cornier than Coco and Chanel, but hey, they had to be distinctive.

They were born from a dog who was rescued from the streets, and they all came to Canada to be rehomed. Again, the breed was unknown, but she really resembled a Norwegian Ridgeback to me. The name Trixie just came to me as I got to know her a bit, so we settled on that one.

Photo by Jacob Ellison. 2020.

The first days are always the hardest, but we developed a system, a schedule, and a mutual understanding. Little did we know Trixie was going to have three weeks of bonding time alone with Jacob. We picked her up at the local kennel on March 9, 2020, and I marveled at how beautiful and petite she was. We knew she was going to be a lot of work because we had never had a puppy before. But honestly, she wasn't any different from the other dogs we brought in from the streets, except that she actually learned quickly with her smart little puppy brain.

Three days after we picked her up, I went on a weeklong vacation with my parents, but then the dreadful COVID-19 came down upon us and we had to quarantine for another two weeks after returning. I was dying to see Trixie the whole time. I had to tell Jacob to stop sending me pictures of her for a couple days because I missed her so much, and it ate away at me to see pictures without knowing when I'd see her again.

I got a couple of good weeks with her before we had to let her go. She came a long way with Jacob when they were alone. She was perfect in every way—incredibly smart with great potential. He was starting to train her to walk beside him without a leash, but that was going to take a lot of time and we never got to finish that training. But she was the only dog we had who could do it. I learned a valuable lesson. Dogs should be rewarded for what they are doing right more often than they face consequences for negative behaviour. If there is no positive reinforcement, the dog will be led to believe that he is always a bad dog. It is so heartbreaking to see a dog who always feels bad and doesn't even understand why. All they know is that they don't have the approval of the one they love.

As we trained her to walk at our side, we would constantly say, "Heel." That was the trigger word for her to walk alongside us. As she walked with us, we gave her treats. As soon as she looked away or started walking ahead, we repeated, "Heel" and gave her treats only when she was obedient. A dog's behaviour can be shaped by giving them a treat whenever they do as they are told or refrain from doing what they've been told to stop. There is so much power in this type of conditioning, as it allows your dog to learn so many new behaviours. Even getting a beer from the fridge. No, I did not try this, but I know someone who successfully did.

Photo by Jacob Ellison. 2020.

Before I left for my trip, she always wanted to chew on something. It was as if she was a teething baby. Well, she probably was. She would stay home alone in the crate because of it, but that didn't stop her. I came home once and found that she had somehow gotten the blanket covering her crate *into* the crate. Then she managed to grab a couple of my dresses hanging in the closet beside her and bring them into the crate as well. There was no escaping it. If I was going to take care of a puppy, I had to accept that at least one of my favourite outfits would be demolished.

In early April, we met with a family at the park. They had two children and a dog but were looking for a second dog. They all fell in love with Trixie, and she embraced them in a friendly and playful way. On April 17, we watched as they walked away with her to their home. I felt horrible because I knew giving her up would break Jacob's heart, but we are very happy for her now that she is living with a fun, loving family that takes her on regular camping and forest adventures.

Photo by Jacob Ellison. 2020.

Let go of what you had, embrace what is here, and believe in what is to come.

Fun Fact: As the article, "Lady Gaga's Famous French Bulldog – Celebrities and Their Pets"

reveals, Lady Gaga appears to be quite a dog lover, having housed four French bulldogs herself. That's a breed I have yet to take into my home, but that squashed face would get many kisses from me.

Not-so-fun Fact: Researchers found that dogs who are negatively trained have more stress-related behaviours than those who receive reward-based training, especially when the reward is food, which they tend to work harder for and respond faster to. This is according to Bryan Lynn's article on *VOA Learning English News*. We live in a society where we have access to so many excellent learning resources on canine behaviour. No matter how many dogs I foster, I will always be able to learn better ways to train and communicate with them.

Chapter Seven: Princess Pepper

My big fat penguin.

For each dog that came in, it would take a day or two to adjust and reveal their true character, sometimes even a week. Pepper brought something meaningful as soon as we took her in. She bonded with me immediately. I had heard that she was going to be a lot of work because she was overweight. I didn't really know what to expect. I suppose I was nonetheless expecting an active dog like the others had been. When I arrived at our usual spot to meet the person who had been transporting her, I was told she would have to be carried out of the car and into mine. The lady opened the passenger door and there was Princess Pepper, like a large pillow, overflowing the seat. I could feel myself getting emotional because she had been stuffed to obesity by her previous owner. It's ironic because they initially named her Princess.

Her previous owner had been about to have her put down because she was too big and too heavy to lift anymore.

I let Jacob lift her the first couple times. We thought she must have been fifty pounds. I found out later she was about forty pounds. We had already had Buddy, who needed to gain weight. Now we had the dog who needed to lose it. Her tiny face had not gained any weight and provided an indication of how slim the rest of her body was meant to be.

She's a long-haired dachshund, which are supposed to weigh between sixteen and thirty-two pounds, according to the *American Kennel Club* Website. The vet said Pepper needed to decrease her weight from forty pounds to fifteen or twenty to become healthy again. If you can't picture how obese she was, just think about Ferdinand, the dachshund from *Tom and Jerry*. I couldn't help but be reminded of him when I first saw her, especially in the food fight scene when he swallows the jello and his body takes on the jello's form.

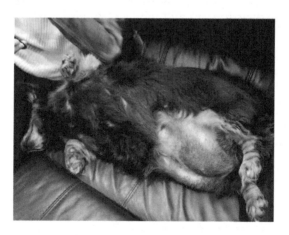

Pepper also reminded me of the living footstool from *Beauty and the Beast,* the way her bum draped over her tiny, stubby legs. My four-year-old niece called her "chunky." We called her "burrito." She was like a massive woolly sausage who walked like a caterpillar. Dachshunds have sensitive spines and, considering all the weight on hers, we made a little ramp for her so she could walk on and off our porch step.

When I came in the house from work, since she couldn't jump, I'd sit on the floor and she would waddle over and lie with her head burrowed into me. And when I started petting her, there was no stopping. When I tried to do something on my phone, her head would make its way under my hand, nudge it, and claim it back. I used to sing the chorus of the Charlie Puth song, *Attention*, to her and declared it her theme song.

She became entranced when I scratched her neck because the poor thing couldn't even reach her own neck with her paws. She twisted her head in weird angles to ensure I wasn't missing a spot. Pepper was mostly comfortable in denlike areas. She always wanted to be under the table where it was cool and covered. She had a great attitude as she became accustomed to our house, and explored it with curiosity. Only she and Roo ever dared to explore our creepy basement with amusement.

Exercise.

Along with her affection and her ability to bond and give complete trust, Pepper was extremely intelligent. She was resilient. She was adaptable to change. She was a great listener, very obedient and intuitive. I made an exercise schedule for her. We spent about 20 minutes every day at *Donegan Park*, a local park in our town. I chose this place because it's mostly grass. With her being twice the normal size of a dachshund with short, tiny legs, and a belly that loosely scratched against the ground, it would have been cruel to exercise her on pavement or gravel. She was extremely uncomfortable all day, every day and needed assistance getting up onto couches, into cars; sometimes she even needed help getting up from a lying position. Her youthful intentions were inhibited by the barrier of her excess weight. She couldn't lie down properly so she struggled to roll on her side. That way she could allow her head to meet the ground. Then I would catch a glimpse of that massive, overhanging belly. I witnessed this struggle just a couple hours after we took her in, and I couldn't wait for her to shed that weight. I was actually worried for the first several nights that she may not wake up in the morning because of how uncomfortable she appeared at night. When she tried to get up to move to the bedroom, the struggle was too much and she would end up staying put. So sad. She was living proof that spoiling does not equal love. Spoiling can sometimes be a form of cruelty.

I noticed that I could no longer habitually walk at my normal pace when I was outside walking with Pepper. Jacob would suddenly say, "Don't drag her!" and my heart would sink as I realized I was stringing her along. Then I couldn't help but giggle every time I looked back to her. She would be trying with all her strength to keep her feet pedaling with the momentum of the leash pulling her—all with a smile on her face, her tongue chilling out the side of her mouth, and her tail perking up.

At times she loved the exercise and wanted to walk despite her hindrances. At other times, she hated it. At the park, we'd walk five feet from the vehicle, and she'd turn her body around and let me know she was ready to head back. I thought, "There's no way, missy. It will take much more than that to make you better." So I pushed her and she would submit. I tried to keep her in the shade, making her trot a few times, then letting her relax. One day, her collar slipped off. She froze and looked me in the eyes, then quickly spun around and waddled away from me, heading toward the car. I laughed and told her she was cute for thinking she could get away with that. I effortlessly caught up and made her finish the walk with me.

I took her for frequent visits to my parents' house. Since it was the heat of summer, the family was always outside. I would place Pepper in the shade under the deck while we all hung out. I wouldn't always tie her up since she was as slow as a turtle and stayed put most of the time. Once I gave myself a heart attack when I went inside for a few minutes and came out to find that no one had noticed that she had disappeared. I ran around the house and saw her, relaxed and halted right beside the passenger door of my car, giving me a clear message as if she were the boss.

Pepper started gallivanting after two weeks. She was a lot more energetic by the third week and noticeably a few pounds smaller on the sides. She would attempt to run, unaware that she looked like a worm bouncing from her rear end to her front. She was mentally ready to jump on and off things; we had to keep our guard up since she came from a breed known for sensitive spines. She jumped off the couch once before we could stop her. Luckily, she was okay but we were cautious after that. After a month, I finally saw her reach and scratch her ear for the first time. Afterward, she shook her head proudly as if she had accomplished a life goal. It gave me great satisfaction to know that our exercising had paid off.

Diet.

When I took her in, she had been on a wet food diet. As a result, her teeth were weak and sensitive. She would not eat dry food, but thankfully, the wet food she was on was supposed to help with weight maintenance. I slowly transitioned her to dry kibble. It was a healthy, weight-control, grain-free kibble. I had to start off making it mushy with water and blending it with the wet food. Eventually, I made it chewier and dryer until she would eat a whole bowl of dry kibble. It took a whole month to make the transition. I was so happy the day she finally did.

She always seemed hungry, and it looked like barely enough food. I knew I wasn't starving her, but I started wondering if I was feeding her just enough to survive. The vet seemed to think so because of the amount of weight loss, which occurred in such a short time. I inferred that her increased energy level was a good indication that she was not starving.

Pepper's social life was great. She approached everyone with enthusiasm and expected them to love her, as they did. She was very observant and intuitive, especially when she acknowledged people as they spoke to her by looking at them and reacting to what they did or said.

She did have a surprising protective side, though. One day, I was sitting in my parents' yard with her beside my lawn chair. My sister's big poodle, Leo, came to greet me. Pepper quickly popped out from behind my chair and bit Leo's mouth. I was surprised she had that kind of fight in her. She was lucky Leo is happy-go-lucky and just pranced away.

One time we were walking at the park and I ran into a lady about my age walking her beautiful and rare-looking dog. She said it was an Australian shepherd and I admiringly said, "Wow, that's what I initially wanted!" She looked down at my flat, waddling penguin with her face kind of sideways, which is when I nervously laughed and said, "Oh, I'm just fostering this one." She eased up and said, "I was gonna say."

Pepper was no Australian shepherd but she had poise, and I will never forget the nurturing relationship we had.

On that note, her greetings were the sweetest out of all the dogs. After two-and-a-half weeks of having her, when we did our greeting ritual, she would weep as loudly as she could. Jacob remarked that she made it seem like he had been torturing her all day and that I had come to her rescue. It makes me laugh to think of how dramatic she was.

With dogs, you can share all your secrets. I'm sure every dog owner has told their dog something they never told anyone else. I have talked to my dogs about my plans and my thoughts, pondering aloud on the couch while petting them. Pepper, specifically, has had to carry the burden of listening to me sing every day in the car on our way to and from the park. It was a song my sister wanted me to sing at her wedding, and I needed somewhere to practice—and someone to silently listen without judgment.

I would get so happy at work thinking about how I got to come home to those whimpers of excitement. But I also knew that one day I'd come home and she would be gone. She embodied hope. And joy. Second chances. She was walking and living proof that what was once corrupted as a result of excessive diet could be restored again with a certain attitude, hope, patience, resilience, and willingness to work for it. At first, she had to be forced, as I would make her get up and push her the extra little bit when she clearly wanted to lie down or go back to the car. But a month in, she was eager. She was running to the car and quick to get up. She was feeling good, and so she eagerly put in effort. And the more she did, the more effortless it became for her. Ten years old and probably in the best shape of her life.

And this goes out to all the dogs, but while watching her progress and become confident and willing to spend all her time with me, and in those soft moments of yearning for me at the door, and in the full trust she placed in me, I knew a mother's love.

To conclude, I want to mention her exact weight. When I first got her, she was roughly 39.2 pounds. By the end of the first week, she was 38, then 36 at the third week, and finally 33.4 pounds on the fourth week before we let her go. As I am writing this before Christmas of 2020, she has been in her new home for two months and is at 31.4 pounds. She is anticipated to be close to twenty pounds by the new year. That is being achieved by all the hard work and dedication put in by her new owners. Her name is Gracie now, they have her on a raw diet, and she receives regular hydrotherapy (swimming is the best weight loss activity because it's not hard on her joints) and even professional massages. Slow and steady wins the race.

The transition to her amazing new home was slower and more difficult than usual. We didn't throw her right into an extended visit; we eased her into it through day visits. It started with her future mom coming over and walking her for about ten minutes every morning. Her first home visit had me heartbroken with no hope, as she whimpered at their door all day and was super happy to see us. But the second day she greeted her new mom excitedly, was eager to get in her car, and looked very confident sitting in there.

Then, she transitioned to eleven-hour home days. Her new mom fed her all meals, exercised her, and returned her to our house for the night. Pepper would race right in our house with her tail wagging hurriedly as she acknowledged us and embraced her familiar surroundings. It seemed like she always had a huge smile on her face. The fifth visiting day, she greeted her new mom with her tail wagging and a bit of whimpering, was lifted into the car and waddled over to the passenger seat, as thrilled as if she was about to go to Canada's Wonderland. The key to a transition with an attached dog is to establish a routine. They don't go through a shock when they experience the change because they have been going through the process slowly. They will have habituated to the new situation, as they were given the chance to taste it, then come back to their home, to familiarity. Taste it some more, come back home. When they are immersed in it, it isn't so new and it easily becomes their new home.

Pepper had so much energy, and she was already a completely different dog from the one we had brought home a month ago. Even though her body was still too big, she was no longer breathing uncomfortably and carrying herself awkwardly as if lugging around a giant tumour. I wasn't emotional like I thought I might be. I knew it was time to let her go when I saw that she finally greeted her new mommy the way she would greet me. I took in our last moments with a full heart. I embraced her for the last time and got to enjoy one more ecstatic greeting the day before. And just like that, I watched her get driven away in that red van. It was the finale of her stay with us and of our profound adventure together.

When those we are close to support and accept us, we are brave enough to be vulnerable and imperfect.

Fun Fact: In the article published on *American Kennel Club*, glucosamine is said to be great for dogs who need stronger joints or who suffer from arthritis. It repairs damaged cartilage to alleviate pain, treats spinal disc injury, promotes recovery from joint surgery, and keeps performance in top condition.

Not-so-fun Fact: Zoe Miller's article also shares that a dog's genetic makeup determines their personality, but as puppies, they are impacted by the lifestyles and personalities of their owners. This is why, if someone leads an unhealthy lifestyle and owns a dog, it's likely their dog will not receive the exercise or nutrition that they need to have a good quality of life—like poor Pepper.

Chapter Eight: Pedro

I thought Pepper would be my last, but after taking a summer break from fostering, I got into it again. By the time I got Pedro, I had already finished writing the previous chapters and was planning on keeping it at that. But just like every other dog, he had some valuable things to teach me. I'll keep it short and sweet.

Pedro was some kind of terrier mix, almost three years old, and from Mexico. I picked him up on October 17, 2020. He wasn't as beautiful as Trixie, with his coarse hair, but he had a very cute face. He was found on the edge of the highway, malnourished, full of fleas, and suffering from respiratory diseases, similar to Buddy. He was extremely excited to start his new life.

Pedro spoke a lot with his face and eyes, which made him very personable. He paid attention to you, looked you in the eyes, and tried to understand your behaviour and cues. Dogs like Pedro are the ones who listen and learn the fastest because they just want to figure out what you want them to do all the time. Pedro always wanted to participate in what you were doing, so patient, gentle, and good-mannered. Even when Jacob yelled at him for chewing a household item instead of his toy, his eyes would divert immediately to mine, as if he wanted to find consolation from me. I fought hard to refrain from reacting. Then he would run into the bedroom and sit on the bed and think about what he had done—or probably forgot what he had done by the time he got there. But after some time, I'd go in there and kiss him softly, and he would feel comfortable enough to come out again.

You heard of Leo, my sister's dog, the "cousin" of all my foster dogs. Pedro was aggressive with him when they met. He lunged at Leo and tried to attack. Pedro wasn't the only one; Buddy too wanted to be left alone by Cousin Leo, but poor Buddy didn't have a mean bone in his body. He would get intensely humped by Leo and look at me with those helpless eyes until I intervened. Pedro didn't need my protection. In fact, he also tried lunging after other dogs when we would go for walks. Once he got sort of used to a dog, he would be okay, and he was extremely friendly with humans.

We kept saying that he was "keepable" because he was such a good listener. He always enjoyed walking or running. Even though I took him for long walks every day, I never felt like I was giving him enough exercise. He was infatuated with squirrels. I often fantasized about putting him on a treadmill with a screen at the edge of it, playing a video of a squirrel running, so he could just believe he was chasing it all day long.

Pedro was the first dog to sleep a whole night with me, cuddled up into a tight ball against my side. He got just as riled up as Buddy when he played. I melted because he always got rough with daddy, biting him playfully, then came to mommy and gave me soft kisses. He also cuddled with someone different every day, but he always chose the person who had spent the most time with him at home that day. It was nice to have someone get as excited as I am about things. I could just cheer and he would get all excited and celebratory with me, wagging his tail and increasing in energy, even though he had no clue what we were excited about.

One morning I was home alone and in a rush to go visit a friend out of town. I was getting ready to take Pedro for a nice walk beforehand. Our door handle was broken, and I locked myself out when I went out to put something in the recycling. I was fighting with the door, panicking. It was raining, and I was in my big fluffy socks, my leopard-print pajama sweater, and my bright red plaid pajama pants. My phone was inside and Pedro was looking at me through the window with a mixture of panic and confusion as I had a meltdown. I tried both doors, and I even tried the neighbor's door for the first time to see if she could drive me to my dad's place; he was the only one with a key, and Jacob was at work out of town. The neighbor wasn't there and I knew my last option was to run across town to my dad's, which would take approximately 40 minutes one way, so that's what I did—there and back. I couldn't help but think what a great workout it would have been for Pedro, but the baby boy was happy to see that I eventually returned. Added to my list of dog training essentials: teach them how to unlock the damn door.

There were a few applications and phone interviews for Pedro, but one lady stood out. She was basically a dog whisperer, and I knew they would love their life together. She takes videos of him running in her big, fenced-in yard, and he is so happy. I met her at the Big Apple venue in the country on November 21. We took him for a walk together and then I let her take him home. It's important to leave a dog in a manner that prevents them from looking at you like you're leaving them behind. Otherwise, they won't have a chance to process the event and they will be heartbroken. I was lucky with Paco in that he was too distracted to notice me leave. But I did it wrong with Buddy, Bentley, and Coco and Chanel. I left them all at the person's house. With Roo, Pepper, and Trixie, it was smooth sailing. So that's one thing I would change moving forward. It's nice to see their new houses, but it's better to let them go in a situation where they will be sort of aloof and won't have the chance to see me leave.

I gave Pedro as many kisses as I could the last couple nights and imagined how much I would miss his happy presence. I also realized he would just add to the list of dogs that make my heart ache when I think about them. I don't know if I can keep doing this! I tell myself I'm done, but then the craving returns…

One of our greatest accomplishments is to bring joy to others.

Fun Fact: When you get a puppy, it's a good idea to take their bones, toys, and food away every once in a while so they don't become possessive. It's much easier for them to learn this as puppies than later in life.

Not-so-fun Fact: Like Pedro, many strays are suffering from sickness or physical impairments. We are the only ones who can help them.

Chapter Nine: The Wolf of Division Street

After my eighth dog, I felt that I had peacefully completed this journey. Then I wanted my ninth, and I thought I was finished. After a five-month break, I just had to get a tenth. As much as I don't regret this because the dog needed help, it has been the most challenging run for us.

His name is Lou. In French (actually spelled loup), it means wolf. He looks like a combination of a Siberian Husky, a wolf, and a starving cayote, with a neck so long he also resembles a goose. He came to us from a pound in Quebec that was going to euthanize him the day we said we'd take him. He arrived to us on April 13 of 2021. He should have been filled out with a big build but instead his body looked like a thin piece of paper. When I ran my fingers across his back, all I felt was a bumpy spine and the grooves of his rib cage along the sides. You could also tell he was malnourished by the texture of his fur, which was long, slick, and delicate without a thick, fluffy undercoat. He had spent his days chained up with a muzzle on and he was severely abused, neglected, and malnourished. He must have been chained on a cement patch as he would only poop on the sidewalk when we took him for walks. To reach his ideal weight, he needed to be fed four cups of food a day. So, I started by feeding him half a cup eight times a day, mixed with a wet food to help him gain weight. The wet food was like a cold stew with beef and veggies in it.

The first weekend felt like an eternity and was one of the most stressful weekends of my life. I just tried to be as calm as I could through everything. He was affectionate which I think was the Husky in him but also very difficult to physically manipulate. He was experiencing all the good things and wanted to take possession over it all. He didn't know how to be an indoor dog. He would growl and threaten us if we were to try to correct him or when he wanted to possess something. Preparing his food was a nightmare as he would get rowdy and jump all over you to try to snatch the food. He was literally starving to death. I learned that the most important thing to do when I feel fear or discomfort is to compose myself as calmly as possible. That first weekend, I found myself constantly talking in a low, soothing voice. I'm not sure who needed that more between me or the dog.

The first few days taught me to be creative. I started preparing his food after putting him in my car, while he was out walking with Jacob, or after tying him up outside. He quickly stopped wanting to get in the car knowing I'd enclose him in there for several minutes. He also made me too anxious when I tied him up outside because he would be so excited to run back into the house that I couldn't untie him fast enough. I couldn't eat in front of him the first week. I'd prepare meals quickly and either eat outside or lock myself in another room.

We thought we were going to get rid of Lou the second night. I sat on the couch with Jacob and he came up and started biting my arm and growling. Then he growled at Jacob as he took his leash to pull him off of me. This was when we knew that if we didn't show him who was alpha quickly, his possessive behaviour would only get worse. The organization advised us to remove his access to the furniture, so we put chairs up on the couch and he was forced to finally use his doggy bed. We put the gate up because he would try to possess the bed and he cried at it throughout the night, peed and pooped in the house, and would jump up on the table. Eventually, we brought his dog bed in the room and he got into the routine of sleeping there quietly near us, although he still tried to claim the bed every now and then.

I had to avoid giving him too much physical affection because he could not be trusted and would start biting or trying to dominate. I usually love when dogs jump on me but I couldn't encourage that behaviour with him. The first time he did get in his doggy bed, we said, "good boy" and he sat proudly with his head in the air. He was starting to submit and listen, and it honestly didn't take that long for him to change his behaviour. We just had to act fast about it. The most affection he was getting from me were short, gentle pets along his worn-down jawline when he would place his head on my lap. Okay, I did kiss him gently a few times on the nose before he left us.

I knew every moment would be about him. I had to move carefully to ensure he was not triggered and so that he knew his place as a dog in the house. When it's in their instincts to be the alpha, we need to remind them who's the boss. We can still be loving and caring yet be assertive enough to establish healthy boundaries and limits.

We broke down a handful of times in the first week of fostering him, trying to plead with the organization to find someone else. But there was no other help for him and there was a whole community rooting for us and raising money for him. I had to remind myself to sympathize with this creature that I intuitively knew could turn on me.

It's crazy how seasons can shift so quickly and how abruptly we find ourselves having to adjust to the next one. Some new seasons are difficult but they are just temporary. I knew I wouldn't even be seeing much of my family with this dog around. Two days in and I couldn't wait to get rid of him, to be completely me and not have to walk on eggshells. He really made me realize how much I would appreciate my freedom when he's gone. But sometimes if you push through the hard times, you can be amazed at how much growth and love you find there. I suddenly and unexpectedly found myself falling more in love with him. Especially when he showed us that he could go against his nature and submit to us.

Perhaps those who survive are not the fittest. Maybe they are the ones who acclimatize to their new circumstances and embrace their changing environment.

Lou wasn't all that bad. He had a sweet, gentle side but also an unpredictable side. We just had to tread lightly. I'm really thankful he was rescued but he needed more than what we could give him. After the first week, he definitely trusted and adored us though. He would actually howl like a wolf in the morning when he greeted us. We had a feeding routine and he would wait patiently as we prepared his food and I would take him to a quiet park regularly so he can explore without the distractions of other dogs. As he got stronger, we used a halti so he couldn't pull us while walking.

Lou had made so much progress in less than three weeks! But then, something started happening. As he was feeling healthier, he was also getting more frustrated and bored around our tiny house. We had finally established order; the walking, feeding, and exercising were all running smoothly, but he started becoming destructive quickly. He had a million toys and was still trying to find new things around the house to tear into. It was when he tore a big hole in the middle of our bed mattress and was ripping the stuffing out that I realized this was the last straw. I had no idea what he would destroy next, when, or how badly. So, on May 4th, a volunteer from the organization came to pick him up and took him to the kennel. It was going to be difficult to find a parent for him who had no dogs and no kids. We feel like we failed. It was a horrible feeling. I just have to trust that he's going to be okay. My dad reassured me that it was only one fail out of ten. And I keep trying to remind myself it wasn't a complete fail. I do believe the progress we made will be carried into his next home experience. He needed rest at first and that's what we gave him. And now he needs exercise and he's in the right place for that.

It's going to take a certain type of person to adopt him. All dogs need to be treated differently. We need to respect the breed of the dog as every breed has a different purpose. His breed is not cut out to be a house dog. He needs a yard with his doghouse. We were very lucky with the experiences we had before him. But fostering dogs is not always a sugar-coated experience. Some dogs will be aggressive. Some destructive. Some loud. It's not easy but I admire the people who are dedicated to the wellbeing of these dogs, no matter what baggage they come with. Some of my family and friends were worried for me. They knew people who got attacked by their rescued dogs. It's for this reason I never tested or challenged him. I did my best and it doesn't always work out. Lou and I had memorable walks and beautiful moments. Even the most aggressive and destructive dogs do have those good sides. But I couldn't give him what he needed. I was in turmoil wondering what would happen to him, but I do hope the right person comes along soon.

Every dog will have its own challenges, some will be a breeze and others will be much more difficult to take care of. But it's a wonderful thing to invite such a disadvantaged creature into our homes and share whatever abundance and prosperity we have to enable them to taste the good life too. This love teaches them to trust again.

Fun Fact: I learned from Cesar's website that a dog is showing signs of submission when they roll on their back to show their belly. Lou started doing this halfway through the first week and it gave us hope.

Not-so-fun Fact: Mitrokostas's article from *The Insider* reveals that flaky skin and fur shedding is a sign of stress in dogs. The poor boy had patches of hair missing on his head, chest, and bum, and very dry, flaky skin all over his body when he first came to us.

I'm sorry, my wolf. I love you.

Chapter Ten: The Mission

Between Pepper and Pedro, we had the honor of babysitting two dogs. The first one was a rottweiler and I was pretty intimidated by her, but she was very sweet. She was at least ten times the size of Bentley and had the opposite behaviour. She wasn't possessive or angry. Then we babysat the most beautiful Great Dane I had ever seen. He was a brindled color, and his body basically took up our whole living room floor. He was incredibly intelligent and good-mannered. He was literally the size of a pony, and I really missed him when he left.

When I foster a dog, I never realize what I'm going to get into next. Roo needed emotional restoration and Pepper needed physical restoration. Both were real-life examples that you can never be too far gone to receive help. And the simple remedy for a dog is a home where love and joy are prioritized, needs are consistently met, and there is lots of patience. There will be even more adventures and lessons that I can't even imagine. That's the mystery, beauty, nobility, and greatness of this experience. And when I reminisce through these pictures and videos, I am reminded not to take any of the moments for granted. I always want to be able to look back and think that I did the best I could and made the most of our time together.

The organization I am with is called K9 Crusaders, founded by Jodi Lane. She has been amazing to work with and her team is wonderful and reliable, but most important, passionate about dog rescue. Her organization is nonprofit, Canadian, and made up of volunteers who support and facilitate animal rescue. Jodi's slogan is "The Voice That Speaks for Those Who Can't," which summarizes the mission of the organization to provide better lives for helpless dogs and cats. The organization partakes in many types of fundraisers to enable them to provide temporary and permanent housing of animals, and ensure that they receive proper vaccinations, microchipping, and other treatments. The organization accepts surrendered animals to prevent families from abandoning their animals, surrendering them to shelters, or rehoming them irresponsibly. Countless animals are rescued from high-kill shelters and pounds. K9 Crusaders accepts foster families to provide temporary homes for these animals until they can be rehabilitated and adopted. Aside from fundraising, the organization accepts donations of animal essentials, including high-quality food, bedding, toys, collars, crates, leashes, shampoo, etc. to ensure the animals are given the best care.

Jodi has business partners in Mexico who retrieve stray dogs and litters from Mexican shelters to provide them with the appropriate vaccinations and treatment for their health, necessary surgery, the right food, and place them in proper foster care until adoption. She takes extra care to place each animal into the best forever home. Many Mexican dogs have been neglected, abandoned, malnourished, abused, and beaten. As such, they require much rehabilitation. I can't explain the suffering they go through, but I know there are haunting, heartbreaking images and videos that the organization has taken when visiting these strays. Jodi has such a big heart for them, and we need someone like her who is willing to turn that passion into action. If you'd like to learn more about K9 Crusaders or donate, visit www.k9c.ca or visit their Facebook page.

Here are some updated pictures of how all the dogs are doing today. Sometimes I run into them. I met Buddy at the park several months after he left me, and he let out a little cry and rested his head in my hand peacefully. I strongly felt that he remembered me, and it was so special. I watched him walk away as I sat in my car with tears making their way down my cheeks. It was just a feeling of loss and gratitude all at once. I had a heavy heart but in the dearest way.

Come on, isn't that the face of a doofus? ♡

Look at that muscle!

If you made it this far, thank you for reading my book. My hope is that I succeeded in bringing you along on this wonderful journey of mine and that you learned some valuable lessons with me. It's easy to let life's circumstances discourage us. But there is so much light along with the darkness and so much to discover if we focus on the many things we all have to be thankful for. We all have our own unique experiences, our own impactful stories, and we get to share them with one another. We get to keep learning. We get to be present in this beautiful life.

Acknowledgements

I want to start by thanking my entire family for always supporting me in everything I do.

I thank my mom, who blurted out, "You should write a book!" when we were walking my foster dogs and I was in the midst of talking her ear off about the interesting life of fostering.

I thank my dad for being the most patient person in the world and being the very first person to edit my entire book and provide valuable insight.

I am thankful to Jodi Lane for allowing me to be a part of this marvelous mission and for trusting me as much as she has.

Thank you to all the amazing parents who adopted these foster dogs and provided them with the prosperous lives they all have now. I am also thankful for their kindness to me and for allowing me to take updated photos of the dogs for this book.

Lastly, I am immensely grateful to my editors for turning my book into a professional work and for believing in me throughout the process.

References

Bryan Lynn, "Study: Negative Dog Training Methods Can Cause Long-Term Harm," *VOA Learning English*, November 17, 2019, https://learningenglish.voanews.com/a/study-negative-dog-training-methods-can-cause-long-term-harm/5166372.html

"Dachshund," *American Kennel Club,* 2021, https://www.akc.org/dog-breeds/dachshund/

Humane Canada. *2018 Animal Shelter Statistics.* 2019. Retrieved from https://humanecanada.ca/wp-content/uploads/2020/03/2018-Canadian-Animal-Shelter-Statistics.pdf

"Is Your Dog Dominant or Submissive?"*Cesar's Way,* November 6, 2019, https://www.cesarsway.com/dominant-or-submissive-which-is-your-dog/

Jessica Barrett, "Mexico's Street Dog Problem — and How Travelers Are Part of the Solution." *World Footprints*, December 10, 2019, https://worldfootprints.com/mexicos-street-dog-problem-and-how-travelers-are-part-of-the-solution/

"Lady Gaga's Famous French Bulldog – Celebrities and Their Pets," *Page A Day*, May 9, 2019, https://www.pageaday.com/blog/lady-gagas-famous-french-bulldog-celebrities-and-their-pets

Laurel Pinson, "The 25 Best Coco Chanel Quotes About Fashion, Life, and True Style" *StyleCaster*, November 21, 2019, https://stylecaster.com/coco-chanel-quotes/

"Mexico Has Highest Number of Stray Dogs in Latin America," *The Yucatan Times*, October 13, 2018, https://www.theyucatantimes.com/2018/10/mexico-has-highest-number-of-stray-dogs-in-latin-america/.

Parnell, "Can Glucosamine Help Treat Arthritis and Joint Pain in Dogs?" *American Kennel Club*, February 17, 2021, https://www.akc.org/expert-advice/health/glucosamine-for-dogs-to-treat-arthritis-joint-pain/

Rebecca O'Connell, "10 Warm Facts About Huskies" *Mental Floss*, December 21, 2016, https://www.mentalfloss.com/article/65600/10-warm-facts-about-huskies

Sheila McClear, "Those Cute Labradoodles Mask a Dark, Disturbing Truth," *New York Post*, September 22, 2018, nypost.com/2018/09/22/why-the-inventor-of-the-labradoodle-regretted-his-creation/.

Sophia Mitrokostas, "Veterinarians share 13 surprising signs your pet could be stressed, and how to help them," *Insider,* July 16, 2020, https://www.insider.com/how-to-tell-if-your-dog-cat-is-stressed-what-to-do

"Why Game of Thrones Success Is Bad News for Huskies," *Burgess*, n.d., https://www.burgesspetcare.com/blog/post.php?s=2017-12-04-why-game-of-thrones-success-is-bad-news-for-huskies

Zoe Miller, "People Have Bonded with Canines for Centuries — and Science Can Help Explain Why Dogs Are Humans' Best Friend," *Insider*, August 16, 2018, https://www.insider.com/dogs-humans-friendship-explained-2018-8#dogs-make-eye-contact-to-bond-just-like-humans-8

Image Credits

All photos are by Anita Corsi except those otherwise cited.

About the Author

Although Anita has a degree in business, she has always been passionate about storytelling. That, combined with her love of dogs, led to this book. Over the course of a year, Anita fostered many different breeds and sizes, in what she calls "a revolving door" for dogs. She lives in a small town with her family, including the three small nieces who make up her world, and she was inspired to write this book while volunteering for K9 Crusaders, her local dog rescue organization.